THE WORLD HERITAGE

AUSTRALIA: LAND OF NATURAL WONDERS

CHILDRENS PRESS®

CHICAGO

Table of Contents

Library of Congress Cataloging-in-Publication Data
Ruiz de Larramendi, Alberto.
   [Australia, una naturaleza singular. English]
   Australia: land of natural wonders / by Alberto Ruiz de Larramendi.
      p.   cm.—(The World heritage)
   Includes index.
   ISBN 0-516-08390-2
   1. Natural history—Australia—Juvenile literature. [1. Natural history—
Australia.] I. Title. II. Series.
   QH197.R8413   1994
   508.94—dc20   94-17017
                                                                  CIP
                                                                  AC

Australia, una naturaleza singular: © INCAFO S.A./Ediciones S.M./UNESCO 1991
Australia: Land of Natural Wonders: © Childrens Press, Inc./UNESCO 1994

ISBN (UNESCO) 92-3-102688-7
ISBN (Childrens Press) 0-516-08390-2

Australia: Land of Natural Wonders

More than two hundred years have passed since the legendary Captain Cook, sailing in a rebuilt coal-carrier called the Endeavour, *first landed on the Australian coast. Australia was then part of what was called the Terra Australis Incognita, or "Unknown Land of the South." Since that time, the island continent has developed a modern, highly technological culture. But Australia, with its 3 million square miles (8 million square kilometers), remains a land of unsettled territories. It has priceless natural areas, unique in all the planet. The World Heritage sites presented here range from exquisite coral reefs to eerie swamplands, from misty rain forests to harsh desertlands. These priceless natural treasures must be preserved—not only for Australians but also for their neighbors all over the world.*

Centuries of History
The Australian continent offers the traveler thousands of surprises. Because it stands apart from other large landmasses, this gigantic island has developed its own unique mix of plants and animals. With its magnificent landscapes, Australia is an open-air laboratory for the study of natural history. Rock paintings in Kakadu National Park *(right)* tell of human cultures possibly as old as thirty thousand years. In contrast, there are immense deserts and exuberant rain forests where marsupials reign. The marsupials are a complex group of mammals whose best-known representative is the kangaroo *(left)*.

Kakadu National Park

Our trip across the Australian continent begins at Kakadu National Park, 100 miles (160 kilometers) east of the city of Darwin. (See map on page 25.) The park is situated in Australia's Northern Territory, in a region called Arnhem Land. Set in a land of profound contrasts, the park embraces the East Alligator and South Alligator Rivers. The waters of these rivers flow through the upper reaches of Arnhem Land into the Arafura Sea, part of the Pacific Ocean.

Kakadu is divided into several natural regions. The highlands, far from the sea, are a rolling plateau. Here and there throughout the highlands are rocky outcroppings. Geologists believe this is one of the oldest areas in Australia. The land is covered with brushy vegetation, dotted by shady woods of a unique Australian myrtle tree. At the plateau's northern reaches, the land breaks abruptly into bluffs, crags, and isolated boulders. This landscape slopes northward to the lower plains, a level region of meadows and eucalyptus forests.

Along the rivers lies an extensive zone of marshy prairies. During the rainy season, the prairies become totally flooded. The climate of this region is characterized by a very distinct annual rain cycle. This swampy region has the park's richest variety of animals. There are important populations of green pygmy geese, spotted crakes, tree ducks, and magpie geese, to name only a few species. The park's coastal zones are covered with tangled mangrove thickets. In some places, it is hard to tell where the shore ends and the sea begins.

From Sea to Plateau
Polished stone axes—possibly the oldest in the world—have been found in Kakadu National Park. There are also exceptional rock paintings. These are fascinating traces of human cultures that flourished here thousands of years ago. Covering 1.5 million acres (600,000 hectares), Kakadu also stands out for the variety of its landscapes. Besides seashores, it has a wide zone of low-lying plains. These regions contrast with areas of cliffs and isolated boulders *(right)*. The floodplains become swamps during the rainy season. These wetlands are a perfect habitat for thousands of birds, such as the anhinga *(left)*. Most of the vegetation in the park is low and brushy.

The thick, spidery roots of the mangroves rise well above the water's surface. These roots form a dense mass that some people have compared with the vaulted ceiling of a Gothic cathedral. The interlocking root system gives the trees surprising stability. These thickets are a refuge for the porous crocodile, which can grow to a length of 25 feet (7.5 meters) or more. This makes it more than 6 feet (2 meters) longer than the Nile crocodile of Egypt. The mangrove thickets are also home to the Johnson's crocodile. This species is seriously threatened by extensive hunting, due to its valuable hide.

Kakadu National Park contains three regions that are intriguing to archaeologists. Here they have found traces of the first human settlements in Australia. They have also found polished stone axes that may be the oldest on earth. In addition, the cliff region has numerous rock paintings. These ancient artworks are remarkably clear. They depict legendary aboriginal heroes, as well as plants and animals. Forty thousand years of history gaze out from these pictures. They help us understand the religious practices and the hunting and fishing techniques of Australia's earliest settlers. They also reveal much about the origins of the culture of Aborigines who still inhabit this land.

Parks of the Eastern Coastal Forests

When the first white colonists arrived in Australia, the southern half of the eastern coast was covered with a dense rain forest. This forest, as much as 150 miles (250 kilometers) wide in some places, covered more than 2.5 million acres (1 million hectares). Its ecosystem is considered one of the most advanced on the planet, comparable only to the ocean's coral reefs in age and complexity. The rain forest owed its existence to the moist ocean breezes that collide with the mountain chain along the coast. These breezes create exceptionally humid conditions and a mild climate with little variation between summer and winter. Unfortunately, this forest has nearly disappeared. Human commercial interests unleashed a dizzying process of deforestation. Trees were cut down for valuable timber, and the rich land was cleared for cattle grazing.

Remains of a Great Ecosystem
Along some 470 miles (750 kilometers) of Australia's eastern coast lie sixteen protected natural areas. These areas, grouped together, have been declared a World Heritage site. They include temperate and subtropical rain forests where many unique plant species grow. The upper photo shows Iluka Nature Reserve, the only coastal zone among the sixteen. Iluka is a unique example of a seaside rain forest. In the lower left photo is Barrington Topsy National Park. On the lower right is one of the protected forests in Dorrigo National Park.

Today less than 15 percent of the forestland, or 310,000 acres (125,000 hectares), remains as it was before the colonists arrived. A continuous green mantle once covered the coasts. Now, along the same coasts, are a few isolated fragments of forest. These areas are separated from one another by farms, villages, and pasturelands. As a result, this World Heritage site embraces a large collection of national parks and reserves. They extend along the coast for about 500 miles (800 kilometers) from Brisbane to Newcastle.

The unique climate of Australia's eastern coast, combined with its rich basaltic soil, makes for a spectacular array of plants. Travelers in the subtropical forest are struck by the thick, humid air. There is also an imposing silence. The light is gentle, filtered through a canopy of foliage more than 130 feet (40 meters) high.

This forest is a type called sclerophyll forest. That is, its trees are species that have thick, leathery leaves. Three distinct levels of vegetation are found here. The upper level is formed by the outspread branches of the tree tops— red cedar, yellow amber, and various types of eucalyptus. Epiphytes, or parasitic plants that grow on the trees, are an important part of this upper level. The middle level is composed of treelike ferns, bushes, and saplings. The lowest level is a tangle of vegetation and decomposing organic matter that nearly hides the ground. Great tree trunks serve as the only landmarks.

A Sea of Coral
The ecosystems on an island such as Australia are not completely isolated. Conditions along the coast *(above)* and in the surrounding waters are important to the protection of natural habitats on the island as a whole. Beaches, estuaries, and the underwater world, especially the coral reefs *(right)*, are seriously threatened by pollution and pressure from tourism.

Special Terms

basaltic soil: Soil containing very hard, greenish-black volcanic rock (page 10)

epiphyte: A plant that grows upon other plants, getting its nutrients from the air, rain, and dust (pages 10 and 16)

paleontology: Science that studies organisms that have left fossilized remains

sclerophyll forest: Forest of trees with tough, leathery leaves, such as the eucalyptus (page 10)

taxonomy: Scientific classification of plants and animals into groups with similar characteristics

The Great Barrier Reef

Green Island *(right)* is a forested coral island in the Great Barrier Reef. The island—16 miles (26 kilometers) northeast of Cairns, Queensland—has been designated a national park. The Great Barrier Reef, one of nature's most impressive monuments, extends for 1,250 miles (2,000 kilometers), covering an area of nearly 116,000 square miles (300,000 square kilometers) along Australia's northeastern coast. This spectacular ecosystem is formed by more than 2,500 reefs. They vary in size from a few acres to more than 40 square miles (100 square kilometers).

One of the best-known animals of this forest is the koala. The koala looks like a teddy bear. It is not a bear, however, but a small marsupial, related to the kangaroo. The koala feeds only on the leaves and buds of the eucalyptus tree. Among Australia's 600 species of eucalyptus, the koala feeds on only 20 species. Until the middle of this century, the koala was hunted relentlessly for its fur. Today it is a protected animal. The image of the koala with its young on its back has become a national symbol for Australia.

The Great Barrier Reef

Imagine a microscopic larva drifting through the ocean currents. It settles on a hard surface in the warm waters along the eastern coast of Australia. Soon the larva changes into a polyp—a primitive sac-like animal with a body less than three quarters of an inch (two centimeters) long. Its mouth is surrounded by a ring of tentacles with which it captures its food. The polyp, covered with a limy outer skeleton, reproduces asexually, forming buds that turn into polyps like itself. Later these polyps produce similar offspring of their own. Soon the limy skeletons of the polyps form a rocklike mass. Tiny worms then bore into the coralline rock, reducing it to a thin sediment that serves as cement for the total structure. This is how a coral reef is born.

Microscopic algae called *zooxanthellae* hover around the coral polyps. A surprising symbiotic relationship exists between these two organisms. The algae use waste products excreted by the polyps, such as carbon dioxide from their respiration. In exchange, the *zooxanthellae* provide starch and proteins that the polyps need in order to form their skeletons.

To establish another coral reef, the polyp uses sexual reproduction. The male expels a cloud of spermatozoa into the water, thus fertilizing the eggs laid by the female. These eggs hatch into larvae, capable of starting the process all over again. When this process continues for many centuries, the result is a magnificent structure such as the Great Barrier Reef. Stretching for 1,250 miles (2,000 kilometers) along Australia's northeastern coast, the Great Barrier is formed by 2,500 separate reefs, ranging from a few acres to more than 40 square miles (100 square kilometers) in size.

Residents of the Reef
More than 1,500 species of fish, 4,000 kinds of mollusks, and about 400 different species of coral can be found along the Great Barrier Reef. The reefs provide a safe feeding ground for the threatened dugong and also a nesting ground for the threatened sea turtle. In addition, thousands of seabirds gather on the islands and islets formed by the coral structure. The upper photo shows a group of pelicans around Cairns. The lower photo shows a spectacular sea anemone, with a fish resting among its tentacles.

In some places, the reefs are separated by channels too narrow for boats to navigate. In other places, the separate reefs lie many miles apart. Seen from the air, the entire structure is breathtaking, with its countless coral banks, islets, lagoons, white sandy keys, channels, and underwater grottoes. The intricate world of the coral provides a home for a multitude of living things, making it one of the most highly evolved ecosystems on earth.

Among all the reef's inhabitants, the fish deserve special attention. Their shapes, their colors, and even their names can be truly outlandish. Examples include the squirrelfish, the brilliant cardinal, the butterfly fish, the angelfish, and the clown fish, to list only a few species.

Many outside conditions threaten the Great Barrier Reef. Contamination from oil and insecticides is a constant danger. In addition, the reef has a new natural enemy that is difficult to control: a starfish, known by its thorny crown, which feeds on coral polyps. It is not certain why the starfish population has suddenly grown. Some studies suggest that overfishing has decreased the starfish's natural predators.

Amidst these threats, the public is becoming ever more aware of the need for conservation. Thus there is hope for the future of the Great Barrier Reef, the largest living structure on earth.

Wilderness Parks of Western Tasmania

Tasmania is a heart-shaped island that seems to hang from the southeastern corner of Australia. The eastern half of the island is covered with green fields where sheep graze, and with leafy forests hung with ferns. Nevertheless, this gentle land becomes wild and inhospitable as one travels westward. The coastline, with its steep cliffs and bluffs, is lashed by rough, gray seas. Bare mountain peaks, sculpted by the ice that once covered this land, rise everywhere. This is a tortured landscape of glacial lakes, canyons, valleys, steep ravines, and waterfalls.

Beyond Australia
The wild reaches of Western Tasmania cover an area of more than 1,800 acres (750 hectares) and preserve one of the world's last great rain forests. Above is a view of Mount Cradle-Lake Saint Clair National Park, shaped by glaciers. At the right is a detail of one of the forest's trees, hung with mosses and epiphytes. At the far right is one of the forest's inhabitants, the kangaroo.

The vegetation consists of impenetrable thickets and the largest temperate forest on earth. This forest is chiefly composed of Antarctic beech, a species also found in New Zealand and Chile. Conifers, eucalyptus, and sassafras are also important.

One of Tasmania's native animals is the largest carnivore (flesh-eater) in this part of the world: the Tasmanian devil. This strange-looking marsupial can weigh up to eighteen pounds (eight kilograms). With a head that looks too large for its squat body, a short tail, and an awkward-looking way of walking, the Tasmanian devil was a bizarre sight for European settlers. Because of its appearance and its quarrelsome temperament, it was given the name "devil." The creature, in fact, is totally harmless to humans.

The platypus and the echidna are two of Tasmania's most interesting creatures. Both are classified as monotremes. That is, they are mammals that lay eggs.

The marsupial wolf of Tasmania is now believed to be extinct. Despite its name, it was closely related to the kangaroo and was not a true wolf at all. It resembled the wolf thanks to a process called convergent evolution. That term describes the process by which two animals that have no relationship or common origin arrive at very similar forms in different parts of the world.

The marsupial wolf fed on small marsupials on the island until colonists and their flocks of sheep arrived. Then its appetite turned from forest animals to sheep, a much easier prey. The rage of the ranchers was boundless. They hunted the wolf until it was exterminated. In 1933, the last known marsupial wolf died in the Hobart Zoo. Since that time, there have been many questionable sightings and blurred photographs of this animal. But no one has real proof that the species still exists. Yet the dense Tasmanian wilderness gives reason to hope that survivors may still be found.

Lord Howe Islands

The Lord Howe archipelago is one of the loveliest island groups in the Pacific Ocean. Though it supports a small human population, it remains largely unaltered from its natural condition. The climate is gentle, with neither tropical heat nor extreme cold. Lush green mountains and dazzling Pacific waters add to its beauty.

Islands Around the Island Continent
Hundreds of islands and islets surround the island continent of Australia. One of the largest is Tasmania, with one of the last great wilderness areas on the planet. In the upper photo is a forest in Tasmania's Southwest National Park. Other islands, though smaller, provide habitats for a great variety of animals and plants. The Lord Howe Islands *(below)* are an example. They shelter numerous native species, especially birds.

Lying some 430 miles (700 kilometers) northeast of Sydney, Lord Howe Island, the main island in the group, is surrounded by smaller islets. To the southeast is Balls Pyramid, a volcanic pinnacle that rises 1,800 feet (550 meters) above the sea. Off the northeast coast of the main island are a group of islets called the Admiralties.

Lieutenant Henry Lidgbird Ball, a British naval officer, found these uninhabited islands in 1788 and named them after Admiral Lord Richard Howe. Soon a small whaling community grew up on the archipelago, but it did not last long.

In the middle of the nineteenth century, a group of farmers settled there, intending to provide fresh fruit and vegetables to passing ships. Later, the hundred inhabitants of Lord Howe turned to the cultivation of a native palm that had become a popular houseplant. Today tourism is the chief industry on the islands.

The landscape of Lord Howe reveals some basic information about the geological history of the archipelago. In many places the islands are covered with volcanic ash. Lord Howe Island was formed by the eruption of an undersea volcano beneath the western ridge of the present-day island. As a result of these eruptions, Lord Howe consists chiefly of rock that dates from the Tertiary Period of the earth's history. The oldest rock is found in the northern part of the island.

The volcano that formed the archipelago is part of an undersea mountain range that extends from the Coral Sea—between New Caledonia and Australia—to New Zealand's Chesterfield Reefs.

The Islands with a Lord's Name

The Lord Howe archipelago is a rare example of isolated islands that were born from volcanic activity more than 6,500 feet (2,000 meters) beneath the ocean's surface. Discovered at the end of the eighteenth century, it has a spectacular topography and exquisite beaches. Here is found the southernmost coral reef on earth. Rich bird life is one of its most outstanding features. Seabirds maintain important nesting colonies on inaccessible islets such as Balls Pyramid, shown in the photo at the far right.

The volcanic activity of this undersea ridge has declined in recent times. Volcanic deposits from the past, however, have made the surrounding ocean waters shallow. Close to the islands, the ocean is no more than 650 feet (200 meters) deep. In contrast, between Lord Howe and Australia, the sea is often as deep as 6,500 feet (2,000 meters).

The soil's rich minerals, plus the fact that it is an island, give Lord Howe an outstanding variety of plants. This spot has seven different regions of vegetation, from tropical rain forests to high grassy plains.

Lord Howe is a natural bird sanctuary, too. The islands shelter important colonies of plovers, petrels, and masked pelicans. They are also home to a highly endangered bird—the Lord Howe's rail, among the rarest species on earth. It is believed that only thirty individuals still survive in the wild.

One final detail should be mentioned. On Lord Howe Island's western shore is the southernmost coral reef in the world. Farther south, the waters are too cold for the coral polyps to survive.

The Willandra Lakes Region

The Willandra Lakes Region lies in the southwest corner of the Australian state of New South Wales, about 440 miles (700 kilometers) southwest of Sydney. It spreads over 1.5 million acres (600,000 hectares). About one-sixth of this region is occupied by ancient freshwater lakes.

The region's geological history began in the Tertiary Period, about sixty-five million years ago. At that time, the sea was receding from this land region. As the waters receded, they left behind important deposits of sand and clay.

These deposits were covered with sand about one and one-half million years ago, during the Quaternary Period. This began the formation of sand dunes in the region.

The low-lying areas were covered with salt water. By a process called leaching, the salts gradually separated out and soaked into the underlying soil. Another factor that helped lower the salinity (saltiness) of these lakes was the inflowing water from Willandra Billabong Creek, which was very low in salt content.

Lakes of the Pleistocene
Mungo National Park lies in a region known generally as Willandra Lakes. A characteristic feature of this region are the basins of ancient freshwater lakes that were formed in the Pleistocene era. Today they are dry. In prehistoric times, however, the presence of water in this otherwise dry land attracted settlements. By studying the remains of human cultures here, we can learn much about the early peoples of the Australian continent. Many traces of these primitive peoples survive among the sand dunes, located along the shores of the lakes.

Chains of sand dunes formed along the lake shores. They curved along the shores in a crescent-shaped pattern. Due to the region's prevailing western winds, most of these crescent-shaped dunes are located on the eastern shores of the lakes.

The lakes began to dry up about fifteen thousand years ago, when Willandra Billabong Creek started to dwindle. One after another, the lakes disappeared. Eventually, the whole basin became a desert.

Glaciers later moved through the continent, but they had no influence in this region. The landscape today is much as it was when the lakes vanished. For this reason, scientists come to Willandra from all over the world. Here they have the opportunity to study the region's former climate and lake structure.

At Willandra, scientists have found skeletons of *homo sapiens*, or modern humans. These are among the oldest skeletons of this type in the world. The archaeological record here spans tens of thousands of years. The discovery of millstones 18,000 years old shows that these people already knew how to grind grains into flour. Traces of funeral rites have also been found. These include a place where bodies were cremated and tombs decorated with paintings in ocher. There is also evidence early economic activity.

Tropical Rain Forests of Queensland

Earlier in this book, we described a wide belt of forests that covered the east coast of Australia before European colonists arrived. That coastal forestland extended from Cape Torres to the land near Tasmania. From north to south, that vast area has a variety of climates, geology, and soil types. Naturally, it also has several distinct ecological regions.

The area we present now was once part of a vast forest that used to cover the northern part of Australia. The plant life in this area is remarkable. So far, scientists have identified close to 1,200 different plant species there. More than 500 of them are not found anywhere else on earth.

Queensland's Rain Forest
Extending for 300 miles (500 kilometers) in the Australian state of Queensland, Australia's last major rain forest lies at the same latitude as the Great Barrier Reef. The fragile rain forest ecosystem is threatened on all of the world's continents. Australia's rain forest has exceptionally rich vegetation *(upper photo, right)*, with some 1,200 plant species. Many of them have not yet been investigated by scientists, and little is known about their potential usefulness to humans.

WORLD HERITAGE SITES

TIMOR SEA

CORAL SEA

Darwin

KAKADU
NATIONAL
PARK

GREAT BARRIER REEF

Townsville

TROPICAL
RAIN FORESTS OF
QUEENSLAND

A U S T R A L I A

ULURU
NATIONAL PARK

Brisbane

PARKS IN THE
EASTERN
FORESTS

LORD HOWE'S
ISLANDS

Perth

Darling

WILLANDRA
LAKES REGION

Sydney

Adelaide

Murray

Canberra

INDIAN OCEAN

Melbourne

TASMAN SEA

WILDERNESS PARKS
OF WESTERN
TASMANIA

Hobart

In this zone there are tropical forests, hardwood forests, salt marshes, and mangrove swamps. They occur in many small, separate segments, some of them miles apart. The plant life in these areas is fascinating. There are primitive plant species growing side-by-side with species that are highly developed. By studying these plants, botanists learn much about the various stages of plant evolution.

The rain forest of Queensland extends from Cooktown to Townsville, some 300 miles (500 kilometers) away. It is at roughly the same latitude as the Great Barrier Reef. This has had an important effect on the conservation of the forest, as the reef is an obstacle to human approach from the sea. Queensland's forest was somewhat protected from the deforestation process that spread inland from the eastern coast. But despite its protected location, the area has been severely stressed.

There are several distinct regions in Queensland's forest zone. The interior is comprised of wide, gently rolling plateaus, where the hardwood forests are found. Nearer to the sea are the coastal mountains. On the other side of the mountains, the land descends toward the sea in a wide belt of rain forest. This section, which enjoys high temperatures year round, is often wrapped in ocean mist. The mist provides the moisture that the rain forest needs in order to remain healthy.

Uluru National Park

In the very heart of Australia, in the middle of Simpson Desert, rises an imposing rocky mass. Its distinct, rounded form stands out stunningly from the level plain. At twilight, when the rays of the setting sun leave the desert in shadow, the rock shines as if it has a light of its own. At that time of day, Ayers Rock, as it is called, burns with a magical red glow. It is not surprising that the Australian Aborigines, who named the rock *Uluru* in their language, treat this spot as a symbol of all creation.

A quick glance at the map reveals that Ayers Rock National Park is isolated from any large human settlements. The rock stands about 250 miles (400 kilometers) from Alice Springs, a medium-sized town in the center of the continent.

Ayers Rock
This national park in the middle of the desert contains the unique monolith known as Ayers Rock *(above)* and the Olga Mountains *(far right)*, consisting of thirty-six steep, rocky domes. The desert melon *(right)* is a traditional food of the region's Aborigines.

It could be said that Ayers Rock was formed by the forces of the desert acting over millions of years. Desert sands were compressed over the years until they formed a hard surface of granite rock. Subjected to extreme high temperatures and very low humidity, the granite broke down over time. Later, erosion wore cavities in its surface. The Aborigines believe these cavities have spiritual significance.

It might seem that animals would be scarce in the desert environment of the Uluru plains. But this is far from true. The park possesses some 150 species of birds, including such well-known varieties as the emu, the bald eagle, the cockatoo, and the parakeet. There are also 26 kinds of mammals and a number of reptiles.

The reptiles vary greatly in size. The tiny skink is only two and three-quarters inches (7 centimeters) long. The *perentei*, a lizard related to the Komodo dragon, may reach 8 feet (2.5 meters) in length. Another reptile of Uluru is the spiny devil, a lizard 6 inches (15 centimeters) long. It owes its name to the spines that protect its skin, from head to tail. When it is frightened, the spiny devil hides its head between its feet, rolling into a great, prickly ball. Its best protection is an impressive spiny collar, crowned by a sharp spear that normally lies along its neck. Its terrifying appearance usually frightens off its few enemies.

Anyone who wants to see kangaroos at Ayers Rock, as at many other places in Australia, will not be disappointed. Besides the little wallaby, the park is home to the red kangaroo, the largest member of the family.

The Great Dome
These photographs show two details of the monolith of Ayers Rock. The rock rises 2,845 feet (867 meters) above the dry plain, and has a circumference of 5.6 miles (9 kilometers). Its smooth sides, pitted by erosion, rise at angles of 80 degrees. This singular dome is composed of sands rich in feldspar. Its spectacular appearance, as it stands above the sandy plains around it, is due to pigments and faults in the rock and to the powerful force of erosion. The Aborigines attach spiritual meaning to the random pits that erosion has left.

Important Dates

1644 The Dutch explorer Abel Tasman lands on the southern coast of Tasmania, then called Van Diemen's Land.

1770 Captain James Cook, in the coal-carrier *Endeavour,* explores Australia's eastern coast.

1788 Captain Arthur Phillip establishes the first British settlement in Australia at Port Jackson; Henry Lidgbird Ball, commander of the steamer *Supply,* discovers the Lord Howe Archipelago.

The Platypus: Bird, Reptile, or Mammal?

In 1798 a strange animal skin reached London from eastern Australia. Experts were convinced that it was a hoax. It had an enormous ducklike bill, the fur of an otter, the tail of a beaver, and webbing between its toes. Sure that they had found a combination of several animals, naturalists armed themselves with scissors and tried to get at the truth. To their surprise, they found that the skin was all in one piece. It belonged to just one animal. Even today, the cuts and incisions in that skin can still be seen. It is carefully preserved in London's Museum of Natural History. Later study of its anatomy led only to further confusion. The animal had the cloaca, or intestinal chamber, typical of birds and reptiles. As new examples of this strange species appeared, it was noted that the females had mammary glands. This seemed to indicate that it was a mammal. But the naturalists were even more perplexed when the Australian zoologist W. H. Caldwell discovered that the young came from eggs with soft, whitish shells. This strange animal, a mixture of duck, otter, beaver, and reptile, was none other than the platypus. Now we know that it is a primitive mammal, an authentic living fossil. Its discovery led scientists to divide mammals into three orders: the monotremes, or egg-laying mammals, including the platypus; the marsupials, mammals with pouches—represented by kangaroos, koalas, and other species; and the placentals, which bear fully developed young—the group containing nearly all of the better-known mammals, including human beings.

The Island Continent

The eight Australian locations listed as World Heritage sites show the continent's natural history in all its uniqueness, variety, and richness. Thousands of square miles of coral barriers, vast deserts, rain forests, ocean islands, traces of prehistoric civilizations, millions of acres of untouched wilderness...each in turn deserves its place among the designated World Heritage sites.

These Sites Are Part of the World Heritage

Kakadu National Park: Set in the Northern Territory, Kakadu includes an ethnological reserve that protects Aboriginal peoples. At Kakadu, anthropologists can study the Aboriginal way of life and its uninterrupted history dating back forty thousand years.

Parks of the Eastern Coastal Forests: These parks represent the last vestiges of the forests that once covered this section of the Australian coast. Made up of a large collection of parks and reserves, it contains some of the most complex and highly evolved forest regions on earth.

The Great Barrier Reef: Embracing Australia's northeastern coast, the barrier represents the planet's most extensive assortment of reefs. Its rich animal life includes 400 species of coral and 1,500 species of fish.

Wilderness Parks of Western Tasmania: These parks include one of the most beautiful temperate forests on earth. The parks stand out for their rugged topography, dotted with steep peaks, waterfalls, ravines, and wild coasts.

Lord Howe Islands: This island paradise is an exceptional example of the results of undersea volcanic activity. It shelters important colonies of seabirds and threatened native species.

Willandra Lakes Region: This region includes the remains of lakes that dried up fifteen thousand years ago. It also contains important archaeological remains and the well-preserved fossils of giant marsupials.

Tropical Rain Forests of Queensland: This area includes Australia's richest collection of plant life. It is crowded with native species that illustrate the evolutionary phases of vegetation.

Uluru National Park: Located in the heart of the Australian continent, the park includes the impressive dome of Ayers Rock, a geological phenomenon revered by the Aboriginal people.

Glossary

aboriginal: primitive; refers to the first of its kind to occur in a region

aborigines: the original inhabitants of a region

archaeologist: a scientist who studies the remains of human life in the past

archipelago: a group of islands

contaminate: to make impure

continent: one of the seven large land masses on the earth

decompose: to separate into parts; to rot or decay

deforestation: the clearing of forests by cutting down or burning the trees

ecosystem: system of plants and animals in one area that function together as a unit

eucalyptus: an Australian evergreen tree with wide, rigid leaves

geologist: a scientist who studies minerals and rocks

grotto: a cavelike niche

humid: having very wet, muggy air

islet: a tiny island

larva: an early, immature form of an animal, still unlike its parent

limy: consisting of lime (a calcium compound) or limestone

marsupial: a mammal whose young are born at an early stage of development and continue to develop in the mother's pouch

mantle: something that covers or envelops

ocher: a red or yellow pigment made from iron ore

polyp: a marine animal with a long, hollow body; one end is attached to a surface and the other end has a tentacle-lined mouth

sediment: particles that settle to the bottom of a liquid

subtropical: having to do with regions that border on the tropics

symbiotic relationship: a relationship of two organisms in which each benefits from the other

vaulted: arched; curved

Index

Page numbers in boldface type indicate illustrations.

Titles in the World Heritage Series

Photo Credits

Front Cover: Pedro Coll/Incafo; p. 3: Angel Ortega/Incafo; p. 4: Alberto Larramendi/Incafo; pp. 5-7: A. Ortega/Incafo; p. 9: A. Larramendi/Incafo; p. 11: A. Ortega/Incafo; Francisco Candela/Incafo; pp. 12-13: A. Ortega/Incafo; p. 15: A. Ortega/Incafo; F. Candela/Incafo; p. 17: A. Ortega/Incafo; pp. 19-21: P. Coll/Incafo; p. 23: G. Robertson/Incafo; pp. 25-29: A. Larramendi/Incafo; p. 31: A. Ortega/Incafo; A. Larramendi/Incafo; back cover: A. Ortega/Incafo; F. Candela/Incafo.

Project Editor, Childrens Press: Ann Heinrichs
Original Text: Alberto Ruiz de Larramendi
Subject Consultants: Dr. Mim Dixon and Dr. James Dixon
Translator: Deborah Kent
Design: Alberto Caffaratto
Cartography: Modesto Arregui
Phototypesetting: Publishers Typesetters Inc.

UNESCO's World Heritage

The United Nations Educational, Scientific, and Cultural Organization (UNESCO) was founded in 1946. Its purpose is to contribute to world peace by promoting cooperation among nations through education, science, and culture. UNESCO believes that such cooperation leads to universal respect for justice, for the rule of law, and for the basic human rights of all people.

UNESCO's many activities include, for example, combatting illiteracy, developing water resources, educating people on the environment, and promoting human rights.

In 1972, UNESCO established its World Heritage Convention. With members from over 100 nations, this international body works to protect cultural and natural wonders throughout the world. These include significant monuments, archaeological sites, geological formations, and natural landscapes. Such treasures, the Convention believes, are part of a World Heritage that belongs to all people. Thus, their preservation is important to us all.

Specialists on the World Heritage Committee have targeted over 300 sites for preservation. Through technical and financial aid, the international community restores, protects, and preserves these sites for future generations.

Volumes in the *World Heritage* series feature spectacular color photographs of various World Heritage sites and explain their historical, cultural, and scientific importance.